MW01114508

ALBERT
EINSTEIN

Gloria D. Miklowitz

⧉ Dominie Press, Inc.

Publisher: Raymond Yuen
Editor: John S. F. Graham
Designer: Greg DiGenti
Photo Credits: Hulton-Deutsch Collection/Corbis (Page 7); Bettmann/Corbis (pages 8, 11, 17, and 21); Corbis (cover and Page 26)

Text copyright © 2002 Gloria D. Miklowitz

Published by:

๏- Dominie Press, Inc.
1949 Kellogg Avenue
Carlsbad, California 92008 USA

www.dominie.com

Paperback ISBN 0-7685-1212-3
Library Bound Edition ISBN 0-7685-1537-8
Printed in Singapore by PH Productions Pte Ltd
2 3 4 5 6 PH 04 03

Table of Contents

Chapter 1

The Nature of the Universe

Albert Einstein was born in 1879 in Ulm, Germany. His father owned a small electrochemical business. His mother taught him to love books and music. Although considered a genius today, Einstein was a slow learner and did not speak well until he was 9 years old. One teacher said he was unlikely to amount to anything.

When he was 5 and sick in bed, his father gave him a compass. No matter which way Einstein turned it, the needle always pointed north. Why? It seemed to him, he said later, as if "something deeply hidden had to be behind things."

His family moved to Munich, Germany, and then to Switzerland, where Albert went to elementary and secondary schools. At 16, his main interest was in mathematics. He hated the military-style classes he attended and was expelled for the bad influence his attitude had on other students. To enter another school, the Swiss Polytechnic Institute in Zurich, he had to make up courses in which he had

Albert Einstein and his sister, Maja, as children 7

Professor Albert Einstein relaxes by playing the violin

done poorly. At the institute, he came to realize that his greatest interest was in physics rather than mathematics.

At that time, scientists faced many disturbing questions about the nature of the universe. With pen, pencil, and paper, Einstein sought answers through the science of physics.

From 1902 to 1909, he worked as an examiner at the Swiss Patent Office in Bern. His job gave him time to conduct his own studies. It also gave him time to sail, play the violin, and marry Mileva Maric, another mathematician he knew from his student days.

In 1905, at the age of 26, Einstein became a Swiss citizen and received a doctorate degree. That same year, three of his papers were published in *The Annals of Physics*, a German scientific journal. These papers later became the basis for a new branch of physics.

Chapter 2

The Three Theories of 1905

In 1905, at the age of 26, Albert Einstein made three of his greatest contributions to science. Each published paper became the basis for a new branch of physics and was written mostly in mathematical symbols.

Albert Einstein gives a lecture to the American Association for the Advancement of Science

11

The first paper, for which he later won the Nobel Prize, suggested that light could be thought of as a stream of tiny particles called *quanta*, or *photons*. The paper, which described the effect of these light particles, would lead to such 20th century advances as motion pictures with sound, television, and many other inventions.

The second paper was about Brownian motion. Einstein said there were tiny particles in water that moved constantly in random directions, bumping up against things and each other.

The third paper presented the special theory of relativity in the equation $E=mc^2$ (energy equals mass times the speed of light squared), for which he is best known. The theory demonstrated that energy and mass could change places, a previously unimaginable idea.

Few people understood the theory of relativity at the time, but that paper and the others made Einstein famous. Historians call 1905 one of the greatest years for scientific discovery because of these three theories.

Universities began competing for him. In the following few years, he lectured and did research at four universities in Switzerland and Czechoslovakia.

In 1914, he was persuaded to accept a well-paid research professorship at the University of Berlin. He also became a full member in the Prussian Academy of Sciences. On accepting the Berlin offer, he said: "The Germans are gambling on me as they would a prize hen. I do not really know whether I shall ever lay another egg."

Einstein's wife, Mileva, chose to remain in Zurich with their two sons. One son, Hans Albert, later became a distinguished professor of hydraulics at University of California, Berkeley. Einstein divorced Mileva, and two years later married Elsa Lowenthal, a distant cousin of his.

Chapter 3

A Deep Moral Sense

Although Jewish by birth, Albert Einstein did not practice his religion. But he had a deep moral sense of right and wrong. During World War I (1914-18) he signed an antiwar petition, only one of four scientists in Germany to do so. It was not a popular action to take. In the 1920s, the rising Nazi party accused Jews of causing Germany's defeat in the war and of being responsible for the country's economic problems. They called Einstein's theories "Jewish physics."

In reaction to Germany's growing anti-Semitism, Einstein became part of the Zionist movement, which called for Jews to have their own homeland in Palestine. He also called for Arabs to have rights in any Jewish state.

When the Nazis came to power in 1933, they launched a campaign against Jews, many of whom were scientists. Einstein and his theory of relativity were particular targets. Jewish university professors were forbidden to teach. The Nazi government took Einstein's property, deprived him of his position and even his citizenship.

Albert and Elsa Einstein in 1922

Einstein left Germany. He came to the United States to take an appointment at Princeton University's new Institute for Advanced Studies. When asked what he thought he should be paid, he suggested $3,000 a year. His wife Elsa, a practical woman, thought otherwise and got Princeton to pay him $16,000. He spent the last 22 years of his life at the Institute.

Einstein became more and more alarmed at Germany's military buildup and its attitude toward Jews during the 1930s. Although he opposed war in general, he spoke up for military action against Hitler. During those years, the United States believed Europe's problems were not its concern.

As incidents in Germany worsened, many Jews tried to come to the United States as refugees, but were turned away. Some said the refugees might take jobs away from Americans.

Unable to change government policy, Einstein still managed to help bring many Jews to America, many of them scholars and scientists.

Chapter 4

The Manhattan Project

With World War II looming in 1939, a group of scientists in America realized what might develop from Einstein's relativity theory. The famous equation that summed up the relation between mass and energy, $E=mc^2$, was the key to a new kind of weapon. They believed it was possible to build a bomb capable of releasing a tremendous amount of energy, an *atomic bomb*.

In Germany, scientists had already started work on this kind of weapon. They had discovered a process called *nuclear fission*, in which energy is created from splitting apart atoms. This energy is the E in Einstein's famous equation.

The scientists in America persuaded Einstein to overcome his opposition to war and to write a letter to President Franklin D. Roosevelt. In the letter, Einstein warned that Germany was conducting experiments with nuclear fission. Along with Einstein, the American scientists wanted the United States to start a nuclear research

At a gathering for the Jewish Refugee Fund in London, Albert Einstein speaks to a crowd

program. Shortly afterward, President Roosevelt started a program which resulted in the secret Manhattan Project. Hundreds of physicists and other scientists were brought together to see if an atomic bomb could be developed. They worked day and night, fearing Germany might succeed at making it before they did.

21

In 1941, the United States entered World War II against Japan, Germany, and Italy. Japan had attacked Hawaii, at Pearl Harbor, and Germany and Italy were already at war with the United States' allies in Europe. With the war going on all around the world, scientists at home were trying to solve the difficult problems of designing and building an atomic bomb.

The atomic bomb was successfully tested in New Mexico in July 1945, just two months after the war in Europe ended. But the war in the Pacific was still going on.

The Allies warned Japan's emperor about the power of the atomic bomb and asked for his surrender. But he refused. In August, 1945, two atomic bombs were dropped on Japanese cities,

Hiroshima and Nagasaki. Japan surrendered a few days later. Over 100,000 people died in the attacks. The devastation caused by the two bombs was terrible, but it brought the war to an end.

Einstein is sometimes blamed for the atomic bomb because he developed the theory that made it possible. But he was not involved in the Manhattan Project and was horrified by its destructive results.

Chapter 5

Everyone Is a Human Being

After World War II, Einstein became a strong believer in world government. He insisted that there could only be peace among nations in the atomic age if all the people of the world were brought together under a single system of law.

"Science has brought forth this danger, but the real problem is in the hearts of men," he said.

In 1952, he was offered the presidency of the new state of Israel, but he turned it down. He felt he was not fit for such a position.

Einstein cared deeply for people who were poor or whose governments oppressed them, and brought attention to their plight.

Much of his wisdom and humor can be found in the letters he wrote to other people. Among them is a description of himself to an eight-year-old cousin in 1920: "pale face, long hair, and a tiny beginning of a paunch. In addition, an awkward gait, and a cigar in the mouth if he happens to have a cigar, and a pen in his pocket or his hand."

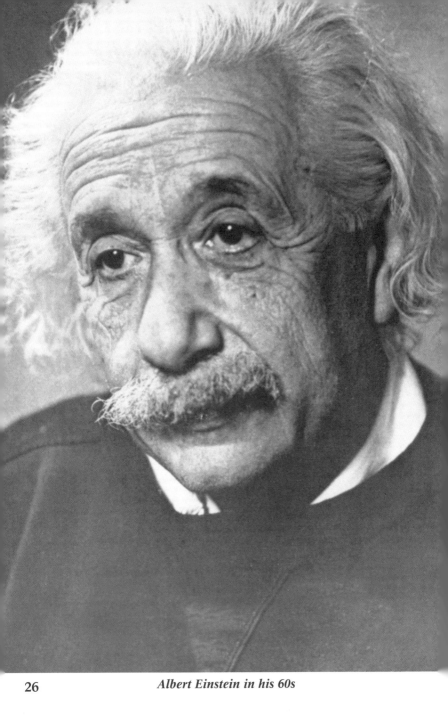

Albert Einstein in his 60s

To an Idaho farmer who named his son Albert, Einstein replied: "Nothing truly valuable arises from ambition or from a mere sense of duty; it stems, rather, from love and devotion toward men and toward objective things."

And, in 1935: "In the last analysis, everyone is a human being, irrespective of whether he is an American or a German, a Jew or a Gentile."

Einstein died on April 18, 1955.

"I am generally regarded as a sort of petrified object, rendered deaf and blind by the years," he confided near the end of his life.

Still, he was so daringly farsighted in his work that only now has the rest of physics begun to catch up.

Einstein was named "Person of the Century" in 1999 by Time magazine for revolutionizing the science of physics. Shortly before his death, scientists in Berkeley, California discovered a new element and named it "Einsteinium" after him. It is in a periodic table of the elements at number 99.

Glossary

Academy - a type of school where one subject or field of study is taught.

Ambition - wanting more than what you have.

Analysis - the information you get when you study something.

Annals - written history.

Anti-Semitism - when people hate Jews or blame them for problems in the world.

Arabs - people who live in the Middle East and western Asia and speak Arabic.

Atoms - microscopic particles that make up larger materials. Everything in the universe is made up of billions and billions of atoms.

Berkeley - a small city east of San Francisco, California.

Berlin - the capital of Germany before the end of World War II.

Buildup - when there is more and more of something.

Campaign - in war, a strategy against an enemy. It doesn't have to be with weapons—it can be with words also.

Compass - a device that has a magnetic needle which always points to the north.

Conducting - organizing and doing.

Czechoslovakia - a small country that used to be in Eastern Europe. In 1989, it split up into two different countries: Slovakia and the Czech Republic.

Deprived - took the rights away from someone.

Devastation - complete destruction; so there is nothing left.

Distinguished - famous and well thought of.

Doctorate - the highest degree from a university that someone can a achieve.

Economic - having to do with money.

Electrochemical - when chemicals are affected by electricity.

Element - a substance that has all the same kinds of atoms in it. Science currently knows about 112 different elements.

Equation - in math, a statement that has equal parts on each side. For example: 2 + 2 = 4.

Expelled - thrown out, usually from a school.

Fission - when an atom has been broken apart, usually releasing energy.

Gentile - someone who is not Jewish; a word usually used by Jews.

Hitler - the leader of Germany during World War II.

Hydraulics - the science of how moving water or other liquids can be used in machines.

Irrespective - without a connection. Usually used: *irrespective of* something.

Israel - a small Middle Eastern country established in the 1940s for Jewish people.

Jewish - a religion. Jewish people are often called Jews.

Lecture - a speech given by a university professor on a topic in class.

Looming - when something is about to happen, usually something bad.

Matter - something that has a physical mass.

Molecule - microscopic particles that make up larger substances. Molecules are made up of atoms connected together.

Munich - a large city in southern Germany.

Nazi - the political party of Germany in World War II.

Nuclear - having to do with the nucleus, or center, of an atom.

Palestine - the region in the Middle East where Israel was established in the 1940s.

Paunch - a slightly fat belly.

Periodic Table of the Elements - a table that lists all of the elements. In the table, they are grouped by their similarities.

Photon - a particle that carries light. When we see something, it is because photons have bounced off of it into our eyes. The sun and electric lights send out photons. They are smaller than atoms.

Physics - the study of matter and energy.

Physicist - someone who studies how the universe works.

Plight - when someone or a group of people are suffering.

Polytechnic Institute - a school or university where students study many different kinds of sciences.

Princeton - a university in New Jersey. It is part of the "Ivy League."

Prussia - a region in eastern Germany.

Quanta - particles that are smaller than atoms (singular—quantum).

Refugees - people who have left a country to escape danger or a hostile government.

Speed of Light - 186,000 miles per second. This is the length of time it takes for light to travel from one point to another.

Squared - when a number is multiplied by itself. For example, three squared is nine (3x3=9); usually written as a small 2, like this: $3^2=9$.

Theory - a statement about something that may or may not be true. Usually, scientists try to find out if a theory is true by doing experiments.

Ulm - a small city in southern Germany.

Zionist - a Jew who supported the establishment of the state of Israel in the Middle East.

Zurich - a city in northern Switzerland.